Insightful Inspirations

Insightful Inspirations

A small compilation of personal poems

A Sluyter

JL Durham

827 Publications

Contents

Dedictation

For Johanna, who insisted on bringing the entire collection of written works back to Pennsylvania after Aleida passed away.

Revisiting these works now that Johanna has passed, it became clear to me that they need to be shared for others to find hope, inspiration and insight.

Peace, Love and Inspiration to All,

Jenny

one

PAY YOUR OWN WAY

We all must pay our very own way.
In every respect
And we should never live
On our neighbors' pocketbook.
Nor should we dump responsibility
On other people's shoulders
But boldy we must accept
Our very own life as ours.

We came alone into this world
Invited by our parents.
They sponsored us for a little while
To show up the ropes of the game.
But once we step out on our own
We take our own fate in hand,
With all its pleasures and problems
WE are in charge alone.

-

A SLUYTER

We all came to this world
To assume a special role
We and we alone
Can truly fill this role.

To me it seems that we must learn
How to create our own pathway
Rooted in the soul's intuition
And guided by the body's instinct

Then we use our brain and mind
To reason for ourselves.
And let the emotions
Tell us when we're right.

We can only hope to succeed
If we stand on our own two feet
Only then are we truly centered
In our very own role.
October 11, 1993

{ **two** }

MENTAL HEALTH

Our mind is like our body
It needs food and exercise
It also must discard its waste
And filter out the poisons.

We must as carefully choose
The food for our minds,
As we choose healthy foods
To keep our body working.

What is it that we need,
And what do we want
To absorb in our minds?
And how do we exercise?

A SLUYTER

To me reason is the exerciser
And the taste will give me choice
I also must keep before my minds eye
The creature I like to become.

Next I must digest my food
Chew it and mull it over,
So that I only absorb in my mind
The qualities I like to keep.
The rest I must speedily discard
Or I will get indigestion.
Which gives me bad rumblings
And pain in the side.

We must also deal with poisons
We better not touch them at all
But if they enter our system
We'd better filter them out.

When we have learned to do ALL OF THIS
We will be in good mental shape
We will be happier and more productive
And on our way to a healthier state.
October 17, 1993

{ **three** }

WORLDLY VALUES

Sometimes we all have the tendency
To compare ourselves with another
But from what angle do we compare
The best side or the worst?

We may feel small or big
Compared to the other fellow
But wait a minute, that's not fair
We measure ears with eyes.

The ear may boost that it can hear
The eye does not hear at all
But the eye can see light and color
The two cannot be compared.

A SLUYTER

We all should be happy
With what we are
We should use our own strength
And do not compare.

We all have many talents
And many shortcomings too
Are we thankful for our blessings
Or do we complain a lot?

What can the reason be for living
Is it not to grow?
To explore new adventures
For further development

Do we really need
Our heaven here on earth?
With no more room for betterment
Just sitting on a cloud?

To me Life is forever changing
Exciting and enjoyable
To be free from the chains of worldly values
That is my goal in life.
July 11, 1994

{ **four** }

RECEIVING HELP

I have felt the help
Others have bestowed on me.
It was often unwelcome,
Not wanted at the time.

I gave myself problems
To be solved by me.
They are what makes me
Grow into a better person.

This does not mean
That help should not be given.

I programmed myself to help
Whenever it is helpful.
And sure enough my impulses
Surprise me time and time again.

{7}

The help I thusly receive or offer
Is quite different from
What my ego would have chosen
Or time wise would select.

Sometimes a smile is all that is needed,
Sometimes money is involved,
Sometimes a little encouragement,
And sometimes nothing is best.

I need to be patient and trust myself
And any other person
We can and should be able
To live the way we choose.
October 12, 2003

five

THE SPIDER

The spider weaves its web
Creating a work of art
It loves to weave
And does it all the time.
To its surprise
It's food just comes along
Just sticking to it's web!

Oh! How I wish I could
Be just like a spider.
With no concern
About anything
Save to create what I like.

I have created for myself
Everything I want.
But that is not the same.

A SLUYTER

I need to change my attitude
Instead of creating for benefits.
It should be just for fun.
The benefits will also come,
As a result and not the goal.

I again look at the spider.
It teaches my just how
To be a successful creator
The way 't was intended for me.
January 18, 2004

{ **six** }

HONOR

Honor and respect
Are basic qualities
I hold in high esteem.
I honor myself
And every person
I come in contact with.

Each person is unique
Each person is divine
Equally to be respected
By all and everyone.

My message to the world
Is who and what I am
That's all I CAN tell,
No matter what words
I choose to utter.

It's what stands behind them
What I really communicate
And that IS me.
The divine unutterable me.

That I am learning to know
By observing step by step
My own communications
Because that is what I think
I am at this moment in my being.

I honor myself.
I respect myself.
I am who I am
And that IS divine.
April 3, 2004

seven

CIVILIZED CONDUCT

What does this mean to me?

It means I honor others
Their property and wishes
And their point of view
I do not use offensive words
When talking, no matter to whom.

It is MY OWN conduct
That I moderate here.
I do not desire anything
That does not belong to me
I do not IMPOSE my view
Or even my wishes on anyone.

I consider it rude.

And so my list is growing.
When I see or experience
Uncivilized behavior,
I add a restriction to my list.

Because that's what I want.

To become the most honorable person
I can envision for myself.

I do not look over my shoulder
Judging myself right and left,
I just state my intention
To myself
That's all that is needed.
The rest takes care of itself.
April 4, 2004

eight

THE ACORN

The acorn contains
The pattern for a full-grown tree.
They are in essence one and the same
Just expressed in different fashion.

The full-grown tree creates millions
Of acorns every year
All contain the pattern
For one unique tree like no other ever

So what do we need
To grow from acorn to tree?

We need a pattern
Condense it to a capsule
Then reach out our roots
And our first tentative shoots

A SLUYTER

All the time the full-grown tree
Is present in our vision

That to me is growing.
From acorn to magnificent tree.
April 24, 2004

{ **nine** }

HUNGER

There is a hunger in this world
Not only hunger for food
But also hunger for love
Hunger for power
And Hunger for peace.

It reminds me of caterpillars
Marching away day and night
Trying to still the hunger
Or quench the thirst they feel.

Some people look for power
Where power cannot be found.
Other people look for wisdom
Where only knowledge is found
Many people look for love
Outside of where it is.

A SLUYTER

Those people leave no stone unturned
To find what they are looking for,
Yet all the time
It has been right where they are,
within themselves.
To be given away
To all the hungry outside.

July 16, 2004

SELF WORTH

When we love ourselves
And are confident enough
To recognize our abilities
And our shortcomings as well,
We are no longer affected
By other people's judgements.

We stand on our own judgement
In glorious self-confidence.
We still should listen
To other people's views of us,
Weigh them carefully
Against our knowledge of ourselves

Then the criticism of others
Can strengthen our self confidence.
July 2, 2004

eleven

OUR DIVINE NATURE

Each person
In all the universe
Is part of All That Is
And thus divine.

Each part of our universe
Is part of All That Is,
Each expressing
In its own unique way
That which is divine.

We all create
According to our nature
Be it beauty, be it ugly
Be it sweet or even pungent.
All is equally divine.

There is a place
For Everything.
A place for birth
And a place for death.
A place to construct.
And a place to destroy.

Each according to its nature.
Each is equally divine.
October 31, 2005

LIVING

We are forever living souls,
Clothed in flesh for now.
To learn the way of the living;
To share and love and live.

Each day we're born anew
To craft a brand-new lif.
Each day we get another chance
To learn and live and love.

Tomorrow is another day,
And yesterday is gone.
Today is all we have
To love and live and share.
Undated